Heaven Declares

Christians'

Greatest Problem

And you shall know the truth and the truth shall set you free! (John 8:32)

Mel Bond

All Scripture quotations in this volume are taken from the *King James Version* of the Bible and Hebrew and Greek Concordances well accepted throughout the world.

Heaven Declares Christians' Greatest Problem
Copyright 2006 by Rev. Mel Bond
Agape Church
140 N. Point Prairie
Wentzville, MO 63385

Printed in the United States of America.
All rights reserved under International Copyright Law. Contents and/or cover may not be reproduced in whole or in part in any form without the express written consent of the Publisher.

Editing:
Caress Bond Davidson
Michelle Forster

ISBN 1-882318-04-08

CONTENTS

Introduction 5

Chapter I

    Legalism 11

Chapter II

    Free From the Curse of Legalism 17

Chapter III

    Wages of Sin Are Still Death 29

Chapter IV

    Knowing What Has Already Been Given 33

Chapter V

    How to Receive Today 37

INTRODUCTION

HEAVEN'S DECLARATION: On Saturday, November 24, 1984 I went to sleep and had a dream that I was in heaven. While I was in heaven I perceived that I should go to a certain home or building and walk in the front door. As soon as I did I saw a friend of mine by the name of Bill Gohring that had passed away a few years prior to this experience. Immediately, he came to me and we embraced.

At this time, we had entered into a building program to build a new church that would seat at least 1,000 people in the auditorium. We were presently renting a storefront building that cost us a little over $1,200.00 per month, not counting utilities or any other expenses. Even though we were averaging around 40 people on Sunday morning, I was so eager to see God's power greatly magnified in an impossible situation.

However, we did not have enough money to pay for our storefront church building's rent each month and were about two months behind. But I was so determined to do something great for the Lord and was really tired of dealing with natural statistics that screamed failure that I set out to borrow as much money as I could to make this new building a reality. I took a list of every name of any one that had ever attended our church for any length of time along with the churches financial statements to several different banks to ask them to lend me the money to build this 18,430 sq. ft. building. Also, Donna and I borrowed as much money as we could against our home that was paid off. The only reason it was paid off was because we literally built it ourselves.

Finally after a few weeks, I was getting really good at giving my presentation on why our church was a good opportunity for a bank to lend this huge sum of money yet still knowing that we had no way of making even the first payment. I had prayed for over ten years to build this building and I was further from getting it than when I started. So I decided that I was simply going to act like God would pay my bills.

Finally, I came in front of a banker that was willing to lend me the money. I can remember the banker looking across from me and asking me if I had a backup plan to make payments just in case we ran into trouble. Instantly, I said, "Sure, my father is rich." Now my earthly father was a poor man that I helped support. However, in my spirit I was saying, "My heavenly father is rich." He did not ask me, so I did not say otherwise and he lent me the money.

A lady in the church offered to buy five acres of land for the building. Keep in mind that this would have never happened if we did not act like God's Word was true. I had been teaching those principles for several years. You will also find this teaching of actions activate God's power in my book "Releasing God's Anointing". So now it was time for me to act like God would meet my bills according to His riches in glory (Phil. 4:19).

Next I rented a bulldozer and started leveling the land for our new huge church building. We almost got the footing in and it starting raining. It rained and rained everyday for a couple of weeks. The weatherman said we had moved into a strong rainy season and it would continue to be like this for at least a couple of months if not more. This was the end of October and in Missouri that is a strong rainy season for us, but this was rare for Missouri. In fact, I have never known it to be as such as the weatherman said it would be. So I was in big trouble. I had signed for all of that money and we were two months behind on the storefront and owed now about $3,400.00 per month on the new building. I began praying as much and as strong as I knew how. Instead of things getting better, things got worse. That's a good sign you're in the will of God. Keep in mind, I had been praying at least two or three weeks and standing and believing God's Word for it to stop raining.

So back to Saturday, November 24, 1984, I went to sleep and had this dream. I saw this friend of mine, Bill Gohring, in heaven. After we embraced, I immediately spoke to him. I said, "Bill, you're in heaven now so you know what is going on concerning people's prayers on earth. What is the deal with my prayers not being answered concerning this rain stopping so I can build our church building?" He said, "Mel, don't worry about the rain that is not the reason you are here. You are here because God wants you to know what Christians' greatest problem is." In my mind and spirit I knew that God was telling Bill to tell me to teach Christians around the world what God says their greatest problem is and how to overcome this problem. Bill continued, "That God said Christians' greatest problem is trying to get to know God or to get God to do something based upon legalistic terms."

Immediately, in my mind, I was not concerned about the rest of the world with all of my trouble. So I said, "Bill, I really do not care I need to know when my prayers are going to be answered and when is it going to stop raining." Bill said, "Mel, don't worry about the rain, that is not the reason you are here. You are here because you need to know what Christians' greatest problem is so you can tell the world. And Christians' greatest problem is trying to know God or trying to get God to do something based upon legalistic terms." I said, "Bill, ok, but when will it stop raining?" He stopped me three times and told me the same thing three times and each time I ask him when will it stop raining. Being very truthful at the time, that was my major concern. The last time after he told me Christians' greatest problem was trying to get to know God or trying to get God to do something based upon legalistic terms he then said, "Don't forget what I said and it will stop raining tomorrow."

The next day was Sunday so Donna and I along with our three daughters went to church and I preached my sermon. It was raining when we woke up, rained all the way to church and rained heavy while I was preaching. Our storefront church used to be a furniture store and one wall was glass from about 18 inches from the floor to the ceiling allowing the rain to be very visible.

I knew I had been to heaven.

Note: As you study the Bible, you will notice that the words *"dream and vision" are interchangeable many times.* The first sermon I preached was on Annapolis Street in St. Ann's, Missouri, at the age of seven in 1957. I have been preaching on a regular basis since the age of 17 and pastoring and doing crusades throughout the U.S. and in several other countries since 1972. I have found from my years of studying God's Word that His highest order of leading and guiding people is first His Word and then perception in your spirit and after that dreams. If you will read the first two chapters of Matthew you will find that Jesus' life came into existence and was saved because of five different dreams. People of the days of Jesus had confidence that God would communicate to them through dreams. God knew that and gave people dreams knowing they would realize He was speaking to them through a dream. They had such confidence in dreams that they would make plans according to the dreams that many times would alter their lives greatly.

Because of people in New Testament times acting like dreams were communication with God, the life of the Son of God was saved. Keep in mind that Jesus is God's only Son and He had the highest of priority in sending Him to earth. So God has a strong confidence in people believing in dreams. Because of people believing dreams that God ordained, Jesus' life was saved several times. Keep in mind that God is the same yesterday, today and forever (Hebrews 13:8).

I will write a book on Divine Dreams soon and you will be able to understand this fact in greater clarity. You can also go to the book of Job 33:14 and you can see a little more clarity on this subject. It reads...For God speaketh once, yea twice, yet man (or woman) perceiveth it not (does not understand or hear His voice). Verse 15...In a dream, in a vision of the night, when deep sleep falleth upon men (or women), in slumbering upon the bed. Verse 16...Then He (God) openeth the ears of men (or women), and sealeth their instruction. In Job, you can plainly see that some dreams are God ordained visions.

Being in Heaven gave me a great deal of peace and confidence. So right in the middle of my sermon I said, "I was in heaven last night and an angel told me (another book I will write will be about some Christians, if not all, after passing away go into the office of an angel as in Matthew 22:30) that it would stop raining today. Immediately, because of the glass wall, everyone turned and looked at the rain simply pouring down. I continued my sermon and prayed for people and then dismissed the people and it rained harder. As I was at the door shaking hands with people as they left, there was one man who was usually critical with just about everything I preached or anything that I would do walked by and we shook hands. He shook my hand with vigor and pushed his shoulder into mine and pointed to the sky outside of the windows and laughed and said, "Mel, it's still raining!" But as he reached out his hand to open the door to go outside the rain stopped and the sky opened up with the brightest sun shining down. The rain totally stopped and it never rained again until our church building was completed.

It was great to experience and see God's power. However, God is more interested in people being free from legalism than He is in any church building. And this was and is a supernatural confirmation that I was in heaven. This was not a mere dream. This was an actual spiritual experience of being in heaven and *it was a supernatural confirmation that God is saying that Christians' greatest problem is trying to get to know God or trying to get God to do something based on legalistic terms.*

So I want to spend some time explaining what legalism is and how to avoid it so we can know God in a closer relationship and we can receive all of God's blessings: spiritually, mentally and physically.

Chapter I

LEGALISM

What is legalism?

Most of our dictionaries will say: Legalism is a strict adherence to the law, especially to the letter rather than the spirit. The doctrine that salvation is gained through good works.

In the Old Testament, God established legalism. Legalism is a law of doing physical things to obtain things from God. God set up legalism so people could receive blessings and needs by their physical deeds. During that dispensation, if you needed certain things you would HAVE TO DO something to earn the blessing.

Legalism is a system of doing things to earn things. There were certain things you could not do and certain things that if you did you would have the curses of Deuteronomy 28:14-68.

If you needed God's power, you would ask God to exercise His power for your needs or desires. Prayers were based upon asking God to do something because of good deeds or agonizing prayers.

In our dispensation today, based upon the New Covenant we have with God, we ask God to show us how to properly use His Word and His power to accomplish something we need to accomplish, or to gain something we want to gain or avoid something we want to avoid. ***There are a host of passages of Scriptures to validate that by God's grace He has ALREADY given unto us ALL things that pertain unto life and Godliness (God-likeness) (II Peter 1:3-4)***. I will not go into detail with this subject as I cover it in greater detail in Chapter V.

Since He has already given us anything we could need, spiritually or naturally, prayer would be communication with the Lord to get His wisdom to help us discover what has been given to us, as well as, wisdom and understanding on how to cause those things to become a manifestation or a reality to us both spiritually and naturally. Ephesians 1:17-18 is a good example of prayer in this area. The Apostle Paul prayed this prayer for the Christians in Ephesus, as well as, many other Christians. He did this by the direction of the Holy Spirit. So I believe it is a divine direction for us to pray it for ourselves today since we are of the same dispensation, the same New Covenant.

I've been praying this prayer just about everyday since 1977 and I've seen the Lord give me insight to Scriptures in many different passages that I've never heard any one ever teach on. This prayer starts out by opening the eyes of our understanding so we may know what the hope of His calling and the riches of His glory (the Greek word for "glory" co-equally is "the reputation of God") to us as a saint of God. I would strongly advise all Christians to pray this prayer every day (Ephesians 1:17-23; 3:14-21). Keep in mind, in praying this prayer you are praying to learn not to earn.

Legalism is a curse.

Galatians 3:10 plainly tells us that legalism is a curse. Verbatimly, this verse says, "For as many as are of the works (the Greek says works is acts, doing, labor) of the law are under the curse.... Legalism is the works of the law. So if we get into works to earn something from God or to get to know God we get underneath the curse. That is why people that get into works are such depressed people and many times very mean people. They really hate their religious experience because the curse is on top of them. This causes many people to be unhappy. The meanest people in the world are those that have a form of Godliness but no power (the Greek word for "power" is "dunamis", which is the miracle working power of God (II Timothy 3:5). The reason they are mean is because they are missing the greatest miracle of all which is being content in whatever state they are in, in Christ (Philippians 4:11).

Galatians 5:4 tells us that Christ is become of no effect fallen from grace. If Christ is become of NO effect to us, then we do not have salvation. If we have no salvation, then we have death living in us. I realize some people are saved and live in legalism, but the reason they are mean or unhappy is an element of death is living in them and that sin of legalism wants more and more control of their lives. James 1:15 says when all sin is finished it bringeth forth death. All sin are seeds of satan and all of his seeds are trying to grow to eternal damnation, eternal hell.

When we try to earn something from God we make Christ of no effect; we violate God's grace, His love, His Word and His gift. Christ is become of no effect unto you, whosoever of you are justified by the law; ye are fallen from grace (Galatians 5:4).

People that work hard for something for many years and don't even get close to having what they are working for are extremely unhappy or angry people, or both. However, some one that does absolutely nothing and in a few days gets given to them everything and more of what the previous person worked so hard for many, many years is an extremely, happy person. They want to dance and laugh because they have been given a GREAT UNMERITED GIFT!

Again, the curse is mentioned in Galatians 3:13.... Christ hath (past tense) redeemed (the Greek says "redeemed" also means "rescued, purchased") us from the curse.... Using different words, Jesus said the same thing in Matthew 15:6 ....Thus have ye made the commandments of God of none effect by the traditions. Regardless of what we've been taught by good people, we must be a people that exalts God's Word above everything else or we will be deceived.

A person can cry and pray all night, but if that person's prayer is not in agreement with God's Word that prayer is an abomination. Jesus said in John 4:24 .....They that worship (the Greek says "to be near to and adore") ***must*** worship Him in spirit and truth. The greatest truth in existence is God's Word. Jesus said in John 17:17....Thy Word is Truth.

A person can do all sorts of things that are good, religious and acceptable by most people, but if it is not in agreement with God's Word those things are useless. Some people think that if they cry and beg God all night to do something that He will do it because of their sacrificing and persistence. However, such prayers are legalistic and useless. Number one: we do not need to beg for something that God has already given us.

Again, I proclaim that God is a good God and He looks at our heart. However, if our heart really is right we will study the Word of God and make changes continually in our Christian mind and life. But *if we do not, it does not matter how long or hard we pray if it is contrary to God's Word our prayers are an abomination.* Proverbs 28:9 says.... He (or she) that turneth away his ear from hearing (being obedient in the Hebrew) the law, even his prayer shall be abomination (disgusting in the Hebrew).

So you can see Jesus saying the same thing with different words in Matthew 15:6....the traditions of men have made God's Word of none effect. Anything that would cause God's Word to be of none effect most definitely would be a curse. And the law was full of hand me down teachings of the past, which are the traditions of men.

Looking at Romans 3:20 you can see the curse of the law by the statement made......By the deeds of the law there shall no flesh be justified in His (God's) sight. The Greek word for "justified" in this passage co-equally means "innocent, righteous and holy". Very plainly, the law was a curse because if a person fulfilled all of the practices and religious acts and rituals of the law, they still could not be justified. Abraham seen into the dispensation of grace that we live in today and applied the New Testament principles of just simply **believing** and he was counted by God as righteous (notice Romans 4:3). (Just a side note: Abraham jumped dispensations because of his great love for the Lord. I could easily write a book about several people in the Old Testament that learned to see and practice future promises of the New Testament and God allowed it. Simply God allowed people that followed Him with their whole heart to jump dispensations. Keep in mind that God has not changed (Hebrews 13:8). We too can jump into the next dispensation if we meet the conditions).

Another passage to validate that legalism is a curse is stated in Romans 4:14.....for if they which are of the law be heirs, faith is made void, and the promise made of none effect. If we live by the Old Testament our faith (trust and belief in God) is made void and the promises of God are made of none effect. If the promises of the New Testament is made none effect, then Jesus lived and died in vain. However, Jesus did not live and die in vain as God's Word is true.

Legalism is a religious system for sinners.

1 Timothy 1:9-10 plainly tells us the law was not made for a righteous person, but for the ungodly; for sinners, for the unholy and profane, for murderers of mothers, for manslayers, for whoremongers, for them that defile themselves with mankind, for menstealers, for liars, for perjured persons and if there be any other thing that is contrary to sound doctrine. The reason for this is people of the Old Testament had dead spirits and could not hear the voice of a loving Spiritual God. All of the people of the Old Testament were sinners by nature. That is the reason we need to be born again. If we are not born again, we think and act like people of the Old Testament.

Legalism is an excellent divine plan and system for people that have dead spirits, which they had in the Old Testament. Some one who is not born again does not understand God's grace. Some one who is not born again can not hear God's voice or understand His perceptions that come to a person that has a live spirit, a spirit that is Christ-like. Notice in I Corinthians 2:14... the natural (the Greek word for "natural" is "bestial nature, principles of an animal, sensual") man (human) receiveth (the Greek word for "receive" also means "to accept, obtain, to get hold of") not the things of the Spirit of God: for they are foolishness unto him: neither can he know (understand) them, because they are spiritually discerned (Greek for "discerned" is "searched or investigated").

Very plainly, you can see by this passage that a person that is not born again would be a person totally directed by their minds, their flesh and the natural courses of this world. Legalism does just that. It leads and guides people by natural senses and natural laws. Legalism is for people that can not listen to the voice of their conscience. If a person is not born again (they do not have a Christ-like spirit) the voice of their conscience will allow them to do things contrary to holiness (Titus 1:15....but unto them that are defiled and unbelieving is nothing pure; but even their mind and conscience is defiled). That is the reason they had to have strict laws that were written down and memorized because the voice of their spirits (which is their conscience) was not dependable.

We see this truth plainly today. When people really believe it is OK to say and do things that are so wrong such as to kill little babies (abortion), homosexuality, as well as, a host of other sins. They are being truthful; they really think sin is ok. The problem is, they are not born again, and their spirits are dead. They have a bestial nature, principles of an animal and sensual nature (notice again I Corinthians 2:14 above).

Note: Christians that depart from God's Word and Christian fellowship (having friends that are non-Christians) and get involved with other sins lose the tenderness of holiness and a Godly conscience. Their conscience gets callused and they begin to think sin is OK.

In I Timothy 4:1-2, the Scriptures teach us that in the latter times some shall depart from the faith (trust and belief in God and His Word), giving heed to seducing spirits and doctrines of devils. Speaking lies in hypocrisy; having ***their conscience seared*** with a hot iron. The Greek word "seared" co-equally means "insensitive". If you apply hot water to your skin little by little and keep doing this for several months you will be able to tolerate and accept several degrees of hotter water than you could have possibly tolerated at first because of your skin becoming insensitive, calloused by the continual application of something contrary to your makeup. When people first sin it is not a good thing for them. However, after several months their spirits become calloused and they accept wrong into their lives. Again, we see that the sinful nature is undependable.

II Corinthians 3:6-7 explains it very well …..Ministers of the New Testament; not of the letter, but of the Spirit: for the letter killeth, but the Spirit giveth life. But if the ministration of death, written and engraven in stones was glorious…….Verse 8……How shall not the ministration of the Spirit be rather glorious? <u>*Very plainly, the Scriptures teach us the Old Testament was of death and the New Testament is of life.*</u>

Again, the Old Testament was a law of legalism for people with dead spirits and the New Testament is a time of unmerited favor for people with spirits that are like God's. That is the reason we are referred to as children of God after we are born again. We have spirits that are divinely alive like our Father God.

Chapter II

FREE FROM THE CURSE OF LEGALISM

In Romans 4:6, the Scripture says....... blessed is the person unto whom God imputeth righteousness without works. The person who reads God's Word and discovers the wealth of their inheritance because of what Jesus did and not what they could ever do is blessed.

This passage makes me think of a prisoner in the United States that has committed horrible crimes but studies the laws of the U.S. while in jail and finds out their citizenship rights and actually lives better than many people outside of the jail who has never committed a crime. In fact, many criminals who are guilty study their rights as a citizen of the United States of America and actually get out of jail. The reason they can do this is because they are a citizen of the U.S. The easiest way to have citizenship rights in the U.S. is to be born in the U.S. with parents that are already citizens. It is never contested. You are automatically a citizen of the U.S. You were born that way.

Many Christians live extremely good lives but are cheated out of the great blessings that Jesus paid for because they do not know their citizenship rights as a Christian. There are several American Indian tribes through out America. To be enrolled (or to be a citizen of that tribe) you must be born into that tribe. You must be born as an American Indian to enjoy the privileges of that tribe. No amount of money can buy enrollment into a tribe, you must be born that way. The blessings of God can not be bought; you must be born into Heaven's Kingdom to enjoy the Kingdom of God privileges. When you are born again you are a citizen of heaven and you have all of the rights of heaven. If you make mistakes the citizenship rights is stronger than the mistake.

Because of the price that Jesus paid, we are free from all of the curses and ill wills of legalism of the Old Testament. Today, we read and study the Holy Scriptures ***not to earn but to learn*** what belongs to us! Keep in mind that the Old Testament is not void. All of the promises and wisdom of the Old Testament are not done away with. We can learn from great people of the Old Testament and glean all of their wisdom and enjoy all of the goodness that they experienced.

Hebrews 7:22 establishes the fact that Jesus made a surety of a better testament. Chapter 8:6 says….hath he obtained a more excellent ministry, by how much also He is the mediator of ***a better covenant, which was established upon better promises***. Whatever God did for any one of the Old Testament, He will do for you and better. If that is not true, Jesus did not need to come and die on the cross and raise from the dead. But thank God He came. And because of His coming and the price He paid we can have all of the blessings of the O.T. In fact, anything God did for any one of the O.T., He will do for us and much more.

Listen to what Jesus said in Matthew 5:17…Think not that I am come to destroy the law, or the prophets: I am not come to destroy, but to fulfill (another word in the Greek to help us understand this verse a little better is the co-equal word "complete" for the word "fulfill"). John 1:17…For the law was given by Moses, but grace and truth came by Jesus Christ.

Romans 7:4 and 6 gives us some plain instructions declaring we are free from the curse of legalism. It reads … my brethren (or sisters), you are become dead to the law by the body of Christ. Verse 6….we are delivered from the law, …that we should serve in newness of Spirit (the Greek says this word also means "Christ's Spirit"), and not in the oldness of the letter (the Greek says this word "letter" co-equally means "Scripture").

Galatians 2:21 ….for if righteousness comes by the law, then Christ is dead in vain! It is impossible to receive righteousness (right standing in holiness, in God's blessings) by deeds. If it was possible, everything Christ did was all vain.

Galatians 3:13…Christ hath redeemed us from the curse of the law, being made a curse for us: for it is written, Cursed is every one that hangeth on a tree. Verse 14..... That the blessing of Abraham might come on the Gentiles through Jesus Christ; that we might receive the promise of the Spirit through faith. Verse 18 ...For if the inheritance be of the law, it is no more of promise: but God gave it to Abraham by promise.

Look at Galatians 3:19 as it explains what I have said previously. Wherefore then serveth the law? (Why was there a law?) It was added because of transgressions (the Greek says the word "transgressions" co-equally means "violation of a command").... Keep in mind, a dead spirit can not hear the voice of the living Spirit of God. A person must be born again to hear God's voice. As we read on in verse 19 it says ..... TILL the seed should come to whom the promise was made..... Verse 22.......the Scripture hath concluded ....the promise by faith of Jesus Christ might be given to them that believe (trust, commit). Who is the seed? Look at verse 29 ... And if ye be Christ's, then are *ye Abraham's seed,* and heirs according to the promise.

Galatians 5:4 ...Christ is become of no effect unto you, whosoever of you are justified (in the Greek "justified" co-equally means "just as if you had it"). By the law (Old Testament works); ye are fallen from grace. If we are fallen from grace, we are then not even born again. This is how strong of a fact it is that we are free from the curse of the law. Plainly, again, you can see from the passages in Galatians we are free from the curse of the law.

Deuteronomy 28:15-68 tells us of the many curses of legalism. Keep in mind that now we are free from these curses not because of our goodness but because of Jesus' goodness. Keep in mind, just because something belongs to some one is not proof that they are utilizing the thing. Or just because some one has something is no proof that they know how to use it. Hosea 4:6 tells us that God's people are destroyed (fail) because of a lack of knowledge. Jesus said in John 8:32 that you shall know the truth and the truth shall set you free.

We must continue to read and search the Scriptures daily to find truths that will set us free and add more riches of God's goodness to our lives. Again, I am saying, read to learn what belongs to you not read to earn.

Acts 13:39 ....by Him (Jesus) we receive justification (the greatest blessings of God), but the law could not give justification. The depth of being free from the curse is strongly spelled out in Colossians 1:22-23 ...In the body of His flesh through death, to present you Holy and unblameable and unreproveable in His sight. God paid the price with His only Son so you would be unblameable. He can not find anything to blame you for. Unreproveable! Jesus paid such a supernatural price that God can not improve on you! You are excellent in His sight. You are Holy in His sight. This word "Holy" is the same word to describe God Himself in I Peter 1:15-16 where He invites us to be Holy just like He is Holy (as well as many other passages throughout the Scriptures describing God as being Holy, Pure, and Perfect).

However, you must read on to Colossians 1:23 were it says......IF you continue in the faith (belief, trust, commitment) grounded and settled, and be not moved away from the hope of the gospel (the word "gospel" in the Greek also means "good news")..... If you will continue to believe, think, talk and act to the best of your ability to this wonderful GOOD NEWS, Holiness, Purity, Perfection, Righteousness then Justification will be yours according to the highest truth in all of existence.

Note: in Colossians 1:22, 23 it says these truths are a reality in God's sight. He will never leave you nor forsake you (Hebrews 13:5), so you will always be in His sight. It's a free gift that was paid for with the greatest price in all of existence. Please make sure it is always in your sight!

Romans 3:28....Therefore we conclude that a man (a person) is justified by faith without the deeds of the law. NOTE: It is very important to know that we are free from every curse of the Old Testament. However, it is just as important to know that you must apply God's Word of the New Testament for it to be experienced. A person that is in prison and is totally innocent will continue to experience the punishment unless they stand up for the laws that will set them free. Many Christians are living below their privileges as citizens of Heaven because they do not know or do not apply the laws of God that belong to them.

I heard a preacher say, "Malachi 3:8-10 (Ye are cursed with a curse: for ye have robbed me (God) in tithes and offerings) does not apply to me because I am of the New Testament. I can not have any of the curses of the Old Testament!" However, this preacher did not believe and did not practice tithing. I also noticed as long as I knew him he always had the curse of poverty and lack in his life. We are free from the curse of poverty and lack if we apply the promises of God that break the curse. If you do not use what belongs to you, it will not benefit you. What good is it to have great blessings that are yours documented by the highest courts in all of existence if you do not believe it or if you do not apply the documents to your case?

Just because God gave us a better way is no sign that everyone will believe it or accept it. In Romans 10:4 the Scriptures tell us ….For Christ is the end of the law for righteousness *to every one that believeth*. The word "righteousness" in this passage in the Greek also means "to have justification, to be innocent, to be Holy". So we are holy, innocent of any wrong doings; we are **_justified if we just believe_**. You are justified if you just believe in God's grace and unmerited love.

Something that is important for us to know is the <u>word "believe" in Romans 10:4</u> has a fuller meaning in the Greek. In fact, this exact word is used 220 times throughout the New Testament. This word is used quite frequently throughout the Scriptures for people to receive great things from God, even to the degree of healings and supernatural miracles, signs and wonders. This word "believe" also means "to have faith in". As you study the Scriptures, you find faith comes from reading God's Word and thinking, talking and acting like it is true (Romans 10:17; James 2:18-20). Keep in mind, in this passage, that "works" is "corresponding actions". The word "believe" in Romans 10:4 also means to "trust". So the more we read and study God's Word the more we can trust God. It also means "commit". We must commit to God's Word.

James 1:7-8 says …For let not that man think that he shall receive any thing of the Lord. A double minded person is unstable in all of their ways. It is not that God is withholding His goodness. It is simply the fact that God's power can not work were God's

Word is not present. You can not run the power of electricity through a place where wire is only some times. You must have a source that can withstand the power. God's Word is the only source that can withstand His great power.

The word "believe" also means "assurance or confidence". I John 5:14-15 says… this is the confidence that we have in him, that, if we ask anything according to His will (God's Word) He heareth us. And if we know that He hears us, whatsoever we ask, we know that we have the petitions that we desire of Him. So this is how you get divine confidence: asking God for things that are in the Holy Scriptures. Notice in I John 5:14, 15 God hearing you is equivalent to God giving you what you ask for.

Plainly, you can see from God's Word that we do not have to fast and pray for forty days to earn something from God. All we have to do is ASK! We do not have to do a lot of religious duties or ceremonies. All we have to do is ASK! We do not have to do anything to earn God's approval to receive from Him. All we have to do is ASK!

Asking

Because we are citizens of Heaven we have some legal rights. One of those rights is the right to demand criminals to leave our property, our families and our lives alone. The word "ask" in I John 5:14-15 co-equally in the Greek is rendered "to strictly demand something due". John 10:10 teaches us the thief (satan) comes to kill, steal and destroy. So we have the authority in Jesus' name to demand satan and his kingdom to leave us alone. We have a right to demand satan to give back what ever God's Word has promised us.

There are 68 other verses in the Bible that give us this same word "ask". Let's look at just a few of them. Matthew 7:7 (Jesus said) Ask, and it will be given you….Verse 8 (Jesus said) …For everyone that asketh receiveth… That's how much authority you have as a citizen of heaven. Matthew 21:22 (Jesus said) And ALL things, whatsoever ye shall ask in prayer, believing, ye shall receive. In John 14:13-14 (Jesus said) And whatsoever ye shall ask in my name, that will I do, that the Father be glorified in the

Son (you are a son or daughter of God if Jesus is the Lord of your life and God is greatly glorified when you are blessed). Then again Jesus said in verse 14...If ye shall ask anything in my name, I will do it. In some translations it renders.... If you ask anything in my name (Jesus' name), if it does not exist I'll (Jesus) make it for you.

When I was in Nicaragua in the year 2000, I was doing a Miracle Crusade in which there where about 4,000 people there. Along with me, were about twelve other ministries from the U.S. I began the part of the service in which I was praying for people that was totally blind. There were two ladies that received their sight. This apparently inspired a young mother to bring her daughter upon the platform that was born without eyes. The little girl was about eight years of age. She was born with some sort of a white substance which filled her eye sockets. I prayed for her and God recreated two perfect brown eyes. Yes, the Scripture is true! If it does not exist, God will make it for you!

Gary Meador, a missionary and graduate of Rhema Bible College, was my interpreter and he watched the miracle take place. I generally close my eyes when I pray so I can focus more in the Spirit. If you would contact Kenneth Hagin Ministries they can get you in contact with Rev. Gary Meador to validate the miracle. Needless to say, it was extremely easy to introduce a loving Heavenly Father that could give a greater miracle; which is to have eternal life (John 10:10; Romans 10:8-10). We had many people to accept Jesus as their Lord in that city because of seeing and hearing about this miracle. I came back about eight months later and the first night in that small city over 1,200 people accepted the Lord in another crusade the first and only night.

Jesus said in John 16:24... Ask (strictly demand what is due you), and ye shall receive, that your joy may be full.

James 4:2 says....ye have not, because ye ask not.

I want to encourage you again to spend time reading, meditating and memorizing God's Word. It makes it much easier to give power that you have. The more power you put within you the more power you can give. Keep in mind, God's Word is His power (Romans 1:16). Again, you read, meditate and memorize not to earn but to learn what is yours. You could also say it this way: All things that pertain to this life and Godlikeness is already yours (II Peter 1:3-4), but if you do not put it in you, you can not use it. It is like nutritional food that some one gives you. If you do not eat it, the nutrition even though it is yours does not help you.

Grace is not neglecting other laws of God.

In this study of learning to lean totally on God's mercy and grace because of us being free from legalism, there is a strong caution I need to make. We must have a proper understanding of reading God's Word, having a strong prayer life, going to church and living a Holy life. We do not neglect the spiritual laws of walking in the Spirit just because we've learned the laws of God's grace. If we do not allow our spirits to rule; our flesh will and we will not enjoy the fullness of life that Lord has provided for us.

Please let me address each of these issues:

Reading: Reading God's Word needs to be in our life continually, NOT TO EARN something from God, BUT TO LEARN. God is smarter than us and He will not reveal everything in His Word to us by reading it just a few times. God's Word is a Divine Spiritual book that can only be understood by the Holy Spirit revealing the truths of its contents to us. It says in I Corinthians 2:9-14…. The Holy Spirit teacheth; comparing spiritual things with spiritual things (God's Word is Spiritual) John 6:63. God will not reveal wonderful blessings and power from His Holy Word if we are not mature enough to receive it. As we read and study God's Word we mature and God reveals more and more of His eternal Divine truths to bless us and those that hear us. So we must read God's Word to learn from God. We should not try and read God's Word in a religious ritual state of mind to try and earn something from God. Keep in mind, God has already given us ALL THINGS THAT PERTAIN TO THIS LIFE AND GOD-LIKENESS (II Peter 1:3-4). You can not possibly earn something that has already been given to you.

Prayer: God is a Spirit: and they that worship (Greek renders "be near to") Him, MUST worship Him in spirit and truth (notice

John 17:17 . ... God's Word is Spirit and Truth). If we do not spend time in prayer with the Lord we will have very little (if any) closeness to Him. If we are not close to Him we can not hear His voice to enrich our lives with His secrets that Jesus paid for us to have. Again, we pray to learn not earn. Prayer should not be a legalistic duty. Real prayer is spending time with the God of all existence that wants to lavish us with loving-kindness that is better than life (Psalm 63:3). Better than anything this world could possibly give. Keep in mind, there are different kinds of prayer. Praying in tongues, speaking God's Word to Him and the type most people know nothing about, learning to listen to God speak to you. If the wealthiest person in the world ask you to come to them and they were going to teach you how to make a few million dollars in the next year. The best things to do are come into their presence and bring a notebook and say very little (maybe nothing). Just listen and take notes. Your heavenly Father has more wealth in every area of thinking than any enity in existence. He yearns for us to come into His presence and let Him enrich our life with His knowledge. Keep in mind, the Lord will always speak in perfect agreement with His Word. That is why we must read His Word. Learn to come into His presence and listen more than speaking.

Church attendance: The greatest manifestation of God in this world is His body which is the church. Ephesians 1:20-23......(Jesus) hath put ALL things under his feet, and gave him to be the head over all things to the church, Which is His body, the FULLNESS OF Him that filleth (fulfills) all in all. The body of Christ has many different members (I Corinthians 12:12-26). The Scriptures give the illustration that it is just as our natural body which has different parts such as eyes, ears, etc. So if you are an ear you need the blessings that God gives the eyes, the mouth, etc. If you are not committed to a local body, you will miss out on most of God's blessings. Even if you are the best ear in the world, you will never be able to see. It is vitally important for you to belong to a good strong Bible believing church; not to earn but to learn what belongs to you.

Hebrews 10:25 plainly gives us another good reason we need

to belong to a good Scriptural, believing church......Not forsaking the assembling of ourselves together, as the manner of some is; but exhorting (comforting and praying together) one another: and so much the more, as you see the day approaching. The word "day" in this passage is the same word "day" in I Thessalonians 5:2 which talks about the rapture of the church (notice I Thessalonians 4:15-5:2). Today, it is extremely obvious that we are very close to the rapture of the church. And very obvious we are closer than people even 100 years ago. So it is vital to belong to a good church.

A foot can be the best foot in the world but it can only go so long without the body before it dies. You may be the best of what God has called you to be, but you will eventually die without the rest of the body of Christ. Not to speak of the fact that the best eye there is, would be a freak if you seen it come down the street looking around without a body. In like manner, we are a spiritual freak if we are not joined hard to a local church body.

Living a Holy life: If we are not living a Holy life, we are living an unholy life. For years satan tricked me into having this train of thought, "Mel, you're not doing or saying something that is sin. Of course it is not a Holy thing you're doing. However, you're just in the flesh." This is a lie that many Christians believe and practice and it keeps them from enjoying God's very best for their life. Romans 8:7 refers to a carnal mind being an enemy against God. So we are either in Holiness or in unholiness. If we live in unholiness, we can not hear God's voice or understand His Word. Our spirits will be blinded (II Cor. 4:4 ...the god of this world (satan) blinds the minds of those that believe not). If we live unholy lives, satan will take advantage of us and we will miss out on many of the promises to enhance our daily lives that the Holy Spirit is speaking to us because our spiritual ears will be dull. Keep in mind, Heaven has greater pleasure than hell. Holiness brings the Divine pleasure of heaven into a natural person's life. We live Holy lives to learn not to earn. Romans 1:4 teaches us plainly that Jesus Christ was declared (ordained) by God to be His Son with supernatural, miracle power ACCORDING to the Spirit of Holiness. Holiness not only is the highest order of joy and completeness in life but it also puts us in a position where God's miracle working power can flow through us easier.

Chapter III

WAGES OF SIN ARE STILL DEATH

It is very important to understand from a Scriptural standpoint, there are only two laws in existence. The law of the Spirit of life in Christ Jesus and the law of sin and death (Romans 8:2).

Even though the law of grace works for us as the means for God's blessings to be made manifest to us in this natural world, in like manner, there is the law of sin and death.

If we have the understanding of the law of God's grace and use it, it will work for us even while we are not perfect or if we have known sin in our lives. A person that has the sin of gossip but has revelation knowledge about financial prosperity and health can be a very wealthy and healthy person. But the sin of gossip will reap wages of not having good friends. So if a person has sin in their life the wages for that sin will come to them but it will not destroy other laws of God's grace that they are working correctly. You can have two jobs that are totally different from each other and earn pay checks from both masters.

At the same time if we allow sin to stay in our lives, we are playing with a seed of destruction. I call little sins; door openers. All sin has a demon behind it and if you allow a demon (a sin) in your life that demon will open the door of your life and let in other demons (sins) that are much worse than he is. Look at Matthew 12:43-45, Jesus talked about a spirit that enters a person and when he does he taketh with him seven other demons more wicked than himself.

James shows us another charteristic of _**ALL**_ sin, when it finally matures it always brings forth death. Look at this progression: 1:14 ...every person that allows himself to be drawn away by temptation, the next step is lust. Verse 15 ...then when lust hath conceived (a person has accepted that sin into their life) it bringeth forth sin. And sin when it is finished, bringeth forth death. James also says in 4:17 …to the person that knows to do good and does it not, it is sin.

Many times Christians are cheated out of a higher quality of life because they allow sin, that is generally accepted by other Christians, into their lives. Romans 8:1-2 talks about the law of sin and death. This law is still in operation today. I do realize if we walk in the Spirit (allowing God's Word to live in our lives) that the law of sin and death can not operate in our lives.

However, just because we live in New Testament times this does not automatically void out the law of sin and death. Many Christians have not and do not have all of the blessings that Jesus paid for because of little sins in their lives.

I want to bring out another very strong doctrine of the law of sin and death. Many times I've known people that really do not care about the laws of sin and death being a part of their lives, because they live so far away from the Lord. But ***the nature of sin (satan) is to kill, steal and*** *destroy the things and the people you love most*, satan is for sure going to make sure people get their wages (Romans 3:23). However, he will always give you wages you do not deserve. I've seen people that did not really care about satan's destruction coming to them. However, when satan gave the wages to their children it was another horrible story.

Look at Exodus 20:5; 34:7; Numbers 14:18; and Deuteronomy 5:9. The Ordained Holy Word of God plainly warns us of another characteristic of the law of sin and death. In these passages of Scripture you find sins of the fathers (parents) being visited upon their children and their children's children.

Another factor about the law of sin is that if we allow even the smallest sin to remain in our life there comes a time when it is too late to do anything about it. In Proverbs 29:1 the Scriptures tell us that God will reprove (correct and warn us of the nature of sin). But the time will come (if we do not get the sin out of our lives) that we will experience destruction without remedy.

I realize I've said some very strong things about the nature of sin. And it is all true. My discourse is not to scare you but to warn you. However, if we will simply focus on the joy and completeness of living like our Father God, then God promises us these passages to be a reality in our lives: I Peter 1:15-16; Matthew 5:48; while living in this natural world (Matthew 6:10). It is such a higher level of life that we will not want to allow even the smallest amount of sin in our lives.

My point in this little chapter is two-fold. Understand the laws of God's grace so you can receive all of God's blessings. And understand the laws of sin and death to know you will still reap the wages of sin if you sin. (Romans 6:23) For the wages of sin is death.

Many people think because many of the laws of God's goodness are working very proficient for them, that God must think the sin in their life is OK, and they continue with that sin. However, James 1:15 tells us that when sin is finished it brings forth death. Some people think that the smaller sins in their lives do not amount to much. And since nobody knows about it but themselves, they continue to live with those sins in their life. But all sin grows to the point of death.

So as we learn to be free from legalism, we must continue to fight against the desires and acts of sin.

Chapter IV

KNOWING WHAT HAS ALREADY BEEN GIVEN

As you study the Scriptures, you will clearly find that we do not have to ask, beg, pray, fast or be good to obtain God's blessings. They have already been given to us. All we need to do is first learn what belongs to us by reading God's Word and then read God's Word to learn how to receive what is already ours. If we do not read and study God's Word, we will be cheated out of the blessings that the Word of God promises us.

I would also like to say if you are not born again you will understand very little of the Word of God (I Cor.1:14). I would also like to say, if you are born again and filled with the Holy Spirit (you speak in tongues) you will have a much more profound understanding of God's Word. First Corinthians 14:2 declares... For he that speaketh in an unknown tongue speaketh not unto men, but unto God: for no man understandeth him; howbeit in the spirit he speaketh mysteries (in the Greek the word "mysteries" has a co-equal word that is "secrets"). And since you speak in tongues, God wants you then to interpret what you have spoken and then you will understand Divine secrets from God (notice verse 13).

Jesus also said when the Holy Spirit comes; He will guide you into all truth. If you have the Holy Spirit living in you with the evidence of speaking in tongues, you have access of being guided and taught all the truths of God's Word. I could easily write a book with Scriptures to clearly support this doctrine of speaking in tongues and the tremendous value of it. If you read any books that I have written, you will notice I do not give one or two Scriptures and then write a 300 page book about those verses. I give many Scriptures on every page to give legitimacy to the true teaching of God's Word.

Study the Word to know what belongs to you.

Hosea 4:6....My people are destroyed for a lack of knowledge.... John 8:32.....Ye shall know the truth, and the truth shall make you free.

All things have already been given to you.

Let me give you a few Scriptures to validate my statements above. John 17:22......the glory (in the Greek the fuller meaning of this word is "the reputation of God"), which thou gavest me I have given them.... In this verse Jesus is praying for all of humanity that believed upon Him up to that point and all that shall believe upon Him until the end of time. Notice verse 20.....Neither pray I for these alone, but for them also which shall believe on Me through the Word (if you will go into the Greek you will notice the word *"their"* is not in the original manuscripts).

Jesus' prayers were always answered. With that fact in mind, Jesus prayed that we would have God's glory (God's reputation). God's reputation is divinely good in all areas of spirit and natural life. We have it now! We simply need to learn how to receive it.

Romans 8:32.....He (God) that spared not His own Son, but delivered Him up for us all, how shall He not with Him also freely give us all things? If the first part of that verse is true then the second part is true also. We know the first part is true. God gave His only Son and He died upon the cross paying the price for us to have a new covenant upon better promises. He died so we could become children of God. The first part of that verse is absolutely true. And so is the second part of the verse, now He has freely given us all things!

II Peter 1:3 ....According to His (God's) divine power hath (past tense, God already did it) given unto us all things that pertain unto life and godliness (God-likeness).... As you read the rest of this verse you see it becomes a reality to the believer based upon their knowledge of God's Word. Any thing you may need or desire in this natural world is already yours. Everything that pertains to Godliness, being like God (a child of God), is now yours. You simply need to learn how to receive what is already yours. According to Hebrews 2:10 by the price that Jesus paid many sons and daughters were brought into glory (this word "glory" is the same as above "God's reputation").

In Ephesians 1:18 Paul prayed for the church at Ephesus that the Christians there would have the eyes of their understanding opened that they would know what the riches of God's Glory (God's reputation) to them as a saint of God is. In verse 19 Paul's prayer went on to pray that they would know what the exceeding greatness of God's miracle working power to them is because of being a child of God. This prayer is not just a prayer for the people at Ephesus This prayer was directed by the Holy Spirit through the Apostle Paul as a pattern for us to use in our daily lives.

Around 1978, I heard Brother Kenneth Hagin say that he seen this Ephesians prayer in the Scriptures and seen that it was a very complete prayer so he started praying this prayer on a daily basis. He said it was not very long that He started seeing and understanding things that he had never seen before. He highly recommended every one to pray this prayer and so I did. I can honestly say the same thing with such strong conviction that I still pray this prayer every day because of the valuable things that have come into my life and continue to come in every area of thinking. The prayer is Ephesians 1:17-19; 4:14-21. Pray it in the first person for yourself.

Ephesians 1:3…..Blessed be the God and Father of our Lord Jesus Christ that HATH (passed tense) blessed us with all spiritual blessings in heavenly places in Christ. In III John 2 God said, "I wish above all things that thou mayest prosper (in the Greek the fuller meaning most definitely is talking about financial prosperity) and be in health even as thy soul is prosperous. Above God being prosperous and healthy, He would rather we be prosperous and healthy.

Notice God says as our souls (our minds) are prosperous. We will have prosperity and health to the degree we are living and walking in the fullness of God's Word. In verse 4 God says He has no greater joy than to know that His children are walking (being occupied with) in truth. Plainly, God desires for us to walk in His Word. And His Word has told us He has already given us all things that pertain to this life and God-likeness (II Peter 1;3,4). God did not say I have no greater joy than for my children to ask me for My blessings. He did say he wants us to walk in it. If you are walking in it then you are experiencing it. Really the decision is yours, God already made His mind up and gave, you just need to receive.

In John 14:6 Jesus said He is truth. He is also the Word of God (John 1:1; 14; Rev. 19:13). Plainly, God wants all of the truths of His promises to enhance our lives in every area of thinking: spiritually, mentally, and naturally.

For your own personal study, I will give you a few more Scriptures to give more validity to this subject. Romans 16:25, 26; Ephesians 3:9, 10; II Cor. 1:20 and Colossians 1:26, 27 ("glory" in this passage is "the reputation of God").

Heaven says, "Christians' greatest problem is trying to get to know God or trying to get God to do something for them based on legalistic terms". You can not earn something that is already given to you.

From a Scriptural standpoint, I've established the solution of getting to know God and receiving from God. You must understand that grace is the channel that allows you to receive what God has already given you. Jesus said in Mark 11:24.....What things soever ye desire, when ye pray; believe that ye receive them, and ye shall have them. Once people discover what belongs to them according to God's Word they need to learn how to receive it.

In this next chapter, I am going to show you how to receive everything that pertains to this life and God-likeness so that it will not only be real in the pages of your Bible but a natural reality to your five physical senses.

Chapter V

HOW TO RECEIVE TODAY

The foundation of receiving is God's Grace. You can not earn God's blessings. It is impossible to earn something that is already yours. As well as, it is impossible to receive anything from such a perfect and Holy God. However, God has made it possible.

God is of a Love that is beyond the natural comprehension. And the proof of this love is His Grace. So understanding grace is the first step of receiving from God. To understand this law ***you must understand the laws of conceiving, accepting, and yielding*** as these words have the same meaning as receiving in the Scriptures, as well as, many times they have the same root word in the Greek.

In this chapter, I will show you in detail these facts I've mentioned and you will know how to receive all of God's promises. Mark 11:24......What things soever ye desire, when ye pray, believe that ye *receive them, and ye shall have them*!

Salvation by grace.

As you study the words save, saved or salvation from Genesis to Revelation, in the Hebrew, Chaldean, Greek and Arabic *every time* the word "salvation" has the same meaning. Which is health, heal (in healing your physical body), deliverance, preservation, safety, make whole (the word "whole" is used in reference to "miracles" such as one missing a bodily part), and prosperity.

Today we receive all of these things from God based on God's goodness and not based upon our goodness.

Ephesians 2:8-9 plainly teaches us that by grace (unmerited favor) we are saved (again this is the same Greek word "saved" as used above) through faith (the Greek word "faith" co-equally means "belief, trust, and assurance"). Verse 9.....Not of works (labor), lest any man (human) should boast. In simplicity, this passage teaches us we have all of God's blessings by His wonderful grace, as we believe and trust His Word.

Romans 4: 3...Abraham believed (not prayed, fasted, etc...) God, and it was counted unto him for righteousness. Verse 5..... But to him that worketh not, but believeth on Him that justifieth the ungodly, his faith is counted for righteousness. Plainly, God's law of grace works for the sinner, as well as, for the saint. Haven't you known of sinners that knew how to work laws of prosperity and became rich? Or sinners that knew how to take care of their bodies and always had an outlook that they would be healthy and they were always healthy (they were using God's laws of health whether they knew it or not).

Verse 6....Even as David also describeth the blessedness of the man, unto whom God imputeth righteousness without works ("works" in the Greek co-equally means "effort or occupation, an act, deed"). The people verse 6 is talking about, are people that have learned not earned God's goodness.

Not just spiritually.

A real good example of God desiring His blessings to be a natural reality, as well as, a Spiritual reality is in II Corinthians 4. In this chapter, God explains in clarity how He desires for His glory, His reputation, to not be just in our spirits but in our mortal flesh. The Greek word "doxa" has its root or base word in the Greek which has a fuller meaning which is "to have the reputation of God". This word "doxa" is used four times in II Corinthians 4, well establishing this fact.

One time it is translated "glorious" and three times "glory". Doxa is used 151 times in the New Testament. Let's look at II Corinthians 4:4.....the god (satan is the god of this world). You can see from this chapter alone that God's desire is for us to have His glory so He is not going to blind our eyes from having it. As well, there is a book to be written to establish the fact that satan is a lower case "g" god that works in this world, blinding the eyes of those who believe not (do not trust, or have confidence in God's Word). And if they would believe the light of the glory (reputation of God) it would shine unto them. Verse 6 .....For God, who commanded the light to shine out of darkness, hath shined in our hearts, to give the light of the knowledge of the glory of God (reputation of God) in the face (fashion) of Jesus Christ.

Verse 7....But we have this treasure in earthen vessels.... The treasure is plainly established in verse 6 which is "doxa". Earthen vessels are the natural bodies we live in. Verse 10......that the life ("zoe" in the Greek which means "life the way God has it") also of Jesus might be made manifest in our body. Verse 11.....that the life also of Jesus might be made manifest in our mortal flesh.

Again, just a few more Scriptures certifying that God has already given us everything we could ever possibly need or desire. As well as, these Scriptures validate the fact that God desires for everything we could ever need or desire to become a spiritual, mental and natural reality in our human life.

Now I want to look at the solution to Christians' greatest problem. Let us get a good understanding how to receive everything that Jesus paid for us to have. Let us get a good understanding how to receive everything that God's Word says is already ours.

Receive and you shall have.

In this portion of the book, I want to show you the simplicity of receiving God's blessings. Every thing God does is simple (Matthew 18:3, Psalm 119:130). If it is not simple God is not involved in it. Receiving is the same as conceiving. Every living thing is alive because of the laws of conception (receiving) of a seed. Every seed must obey the laws of itself or it will never develop into what that seed promises. You can not put a seed of an apple into a monkey and get an apple monkey. All of God's Word is Spiritual seeds of God and if we will follow the laws of each seed we will have what it says we can have.

Example: I Peter 2:24 says I am healed already. If I want to have that truth as a reality in the natural world I must obey the laws of that seed. First, I must believe that seed is true. Second, I must yield (surrender, get in a relaxed state of receiving). Third, I must talk like it is true. Finally, I must act like that seed is true. If we will follow these basic principles in planting any kind of natural seed, we will reap a harvest.

Now in the remainder of this chapter I am going to go into greater depths validating what I said in this introduction.

Receiving is conceiving.

I Peter 1:23 confirms one of the strongest doctrines in the Holy Scriptures: being born-again. This doctrine is established by the seed of God's Word. A person can not be saved; can not be a true child of God unless they have God's seed for the new birth conceived in their spirit. (I Peter 1:23….Being born again, not of corruptible ("perishable" in the Greek) seed, but of incorruptible, by the Word of God….. By looking at this passage, as well as, the Greek, you can plainly see the corruptible seed mentioned in this passage is in reference to the natural seed of humanity and the Spiritual seed is God's Word.

In Luke 1:24; 31; 36; 2:21 the word "conceive" is used in reference to the mother of John the Baptist conceiving John and Mary, the mother of Jesus, conceiving Jesus. The word "conceive" in these passages have the basic same meaning in the Greek as the word "receive" in Mark 11:24 and many other passages where the word "receive" is used. The Greek word "conceive" in the passages mentioned also *comes from the word "receive"* in the Greek.

You will also notice looking in most dictionaries that both words have the basic same meanings. Understanding this we can better understand Mark 11:24 when Jesus told us that what things soever we desire when we pray if we will first receive (conceive God's Word; God's seed for that promise) we will have. *When that seed has fully matured to the point that it can live outside of our spirits, then we will have it in the natural world.*

The seed must fulfill its full gestation period in our spirits first. Many people get pregnant with the seed of God's Word but because of circumstances or because there is not a natural manifestation in their time frame they abort God's seed. Just as all seeds have different gestation periods so do the many, many different types of seeds of God. God has a different seed promise for every thing you could possibly need or desire in this life, as well as, the life to come.

Believing is part of conceiving.

If you do not believe in the seed you will never have what the seed promises. A wheat seed promises you wheat and you must believe in what that seed promises. The first step of believing in a seed is accepting it in your mind that the seed is real, that it is telling the truth. That it can produce what it says it can produce. As long as you accept in your mind the promise of what the seed says, you have a strong foundation of conceiving the seed. When a person truly believes in a seed they will have mental pictures of seeing that seed in full maturity where their senses can relate to it.

God's Words are His seeds and we must obey these same laws for conceiving God's seeds. In Proverbs 29:18 the Bible strongly talks about conceiving the seeds of God using different words. The Scripture says, "Where there is no vision, the people perish: but he that keepeth the law, happy is he. Notice the truth of this passage: if you keep the law (which in the Hebrew is "Divine Instructions") you will be happy. And if you are keeping God's Word you then are clearly having visions. The Hebrew word for "vision" in this passage clearly deals with believing God's Word strongly. In the Hebrew it says, "To mentally have a dream, especially to have a vision, mentally dream an oracle or a revelation, to bind firmly. As you study the word "oracle" you find that an oracle of God is the strongest mandate, desire that God has. If God issues a oracle there is absolutely nothing that can stop it. A mandate was when God said, "Let there be light". Darkness had to leave, regardless of how impossible it was for light to be in existence.

Look clearly at this verse again. When we take God's Word (that is a clear doctrine of God) there are at least three passages of Scripture saying the same thing. The passages are in agreement with the chapter and the rest of the Bible and it clearly glorifies God (you have a strong doctrine of God) and you mentally, purposely have a dream; you are especially have a mental dream. You are in the highest order, having an ORACLE OF GOD. You are having the highest order of visions. If you KEEP the vision you will be happy and instead of the promise perishing from you, it will come to pass in the natural world.

Talking is part of conceiving.
If you want what a natural seed promises you must talk about

it a lot. If you want a flower garden you will talk to a lot of people about that kind of seed. Where can I buy that kind of seed? When, where, and how to plant that seed and how to care for it. You will do more talking about that seed then you may possibly realize. Talking is an extremely important part of conceiving any seed.

I understand that God is a fair God and some people at the present time may not be able to audibly talk. However, they will get the information that I have covered in this section communicated to them in some way until they understand. So they can have the conception of the seed that they want to mature in their life and God will honor that. God's seeds must be talked about also and it is extremely Scriptural.

You will notice Jesus said in Mark 11:23 that we could have whatsoever we said (of course when speaking in agreement with God's Word). Brother Kenneth Hagin mentioned that Jesus appeared to him and told him to notice in this passage that "saying" is mentioned three times where "believing" is only mentioned once. Brother Hagin has a mini book that will change your life if you believe in the Scriptures in that book. It is titled *"You Can Have Whatsoever You Say!"*

You will notice that is the way God thinks. That is the way God does things. In the very beginning of this world **_GOD SAID_** fourteen times in the first chapter of Genesis and each time there was a manifestation. In Romans 4:17 it says....God, who quickeneth the dead, and calleth those things which be not as though they were. Romans was repeating what took place in Genesis 17:1 and 5 when God spoke to Abraham when he was 99 years old. God called him "the father of many nations" when it was impossible for Abraham to father a child and his wife Sarah to conceive when she was 90 years old (Genesis 17:17).

Romans 4:23-24 states.... Now it was not written for his sake alone, that it was imputed (spoken) to him; But for us also, to whom it shall be imputed, if we believe..... Here are just a few more passages for your personal study to validate that talking about your seed is a vital part of conceiving the seeds of God's Word. (Matt. 21:21 and 37; Luke 17:6; Hebrews 11:3; Prov. 6:2; 14:3; 18:21; 21:23)

Yielding is part of conceiving.

If you break the law of yielding you will never have in the natural, what a seed promises. The word "yield" from a Scriptural standpoint has the same meaning as "relaxing". If you want a seed to conceive you must put it in a very relaxed state. But if you instead worry that the seed might not come up, put too much water or fertilizer on the seed, or mess with the ground the seed will most likely die. Like yielding, relaxing is an extremely important part of conceiving God's Word.

Moses conceived a miracle from God in Exodus 14:13. God told Moses to stand still and He would see the salvation of God. The word "stand" in the Hebrew is also rendered "reflexively", which is relaxing. Moses saw the 1,700 feet of water stand up on each side as a wall, the bottom of the sea was dry ground and two million of God's people walked through the midst of the sea. Very apparent, Moses had relaxed to conceive and then he had a miracle of God. Keep in mind, many of God's seeds can manifest instantly. However, do not be discouraged as some seeds may take longer. There are some natural seeds, which I know of, that involve many years of gestation.

Isaiah 30:7.....their strength is to sit still (rest). Ephesians 6:13-14.....having done all to stand (when you have done all that you know to do in the doing of God's Word) stand (the word "stand" in the Greek co-equally is "rest").

Romans 6:19 declares that just as simple as you have yielded your flesh to unholiness in the same manner now yield (the Greek word for "yield" is also rendered "reflexive, utterly prostrate, conceive, lay down") to Holiness. Note: Holiness in this passage is the same word for Holiness in I Peter 1:15-16 where God invites us to be as holy as He is. This word "holy" is also rendered co-equally in the Greek as "pure, blameless, perfect, innocent, and clean".

Keep this in mind, God is more powerful than the devil and it is extremely easy to yield to satan. However, since God is more powerful than satan, it is even more easier to yield to God. When you yield to God, you yield to His pureness, blamelessness, perfection, and innocence. If God's Word promises you something, simply relax and yield to it. Yield to being innocent of any ill will or defeat; it's easier than sin.

I Thessalonians 4:11-12.....study to be quiet (in the Greek the word "quiet" is also rendered "rest, to keep still") …..that you may lack of nothing. In Hebrews 3:19 and 4:1 God's people could not enter into God's blessings because they would not relax. God said in 4:3 that those that enter His blessings enter in because they learned to relax. Verse 9 says….There remaineth therefore a rest to the people of God. Then 4:11 tells us how to enter into that rest of God, which is labor. This word in the Greek is rendered also to make an effort; to study. If you were stranded out in the sea and there wasn't land in sight in any direction. If you knew the true direction there would be a great deal of relaxing in your life even though you are producing a lot of energy to get there. However, there is only one way and all the other directions take you out into the depths of the sea.

When we study God's Word, there comes a supernatural confidence that causes us to relax and be at peace even in the worst situations. (I John 5:14, 15..….And this is the confidence that we have in Him, that, if we ask any thing according to His will (His will is His Word), He heareth us. And if we know that He hears us, whatsoever we ask, WE KNOW WE HAVE….!

Acting is part of conceiving.

Again, if you obey the natural laws of a natural seed you must have some physical actions or you will never fully conceive the seed. You *must* have actions. Your actions for a natural seed would be many; such as going to several stores: to buy the seeds, tools, fertilizer, etc…. Then you would have a lot of actions with all of the things that you bought. With God's seeds there must be actions also. Actions will activate God's power. Actions are the last thing that a person must do in conceiving God's Word before they have what it says in the natural.

James 2:19 states…..Thou believest that there is one God; thou doest well: the devils also believe, and tremble. Verse 20…. faith without works is dead. "Works" in this passage is rendered in the Greek as "actions". If we believe but do not have any corresponding actions our belief, our faith is the same as the devils of hell. If a person truly believes the Word of God they will act like God's Word is true.

Let me give you a few Scriptures to show you when people believed God's Word and then acted on it that it activated God's power and they had in the natural what it says in the Spiritual. Matthew 9:20 and 22......a woman, which was diseased with an issue of blood twelve years, came behind him, touched the hem of His garment and was instantly healed. Notice the hem of Jesus' garment was near the ground and there was a great crowd around Jesus. The woman was extremely weak as she had the disease twelve years. Clearly she had a lot of natural actions that activated God's miracle power.

Matthew 14.....Peter got out of the boat to walk on the water. He acted like Jesus was telling him the truth. Keep in mind, all of God's Word is truth. Mark 10:50...blind Bartimaeus threw his government license (his cloak) to beg, away and came to Jesus. Bartimaeus did all of this while he was still blind. His actions activated God's miracle power. In John 5:5-8 the man was totally paralyzed for 38 years, but when he made all efforts to walk (believing God's Word), then he walked.

Mark 9:23...All things are possible to those that believe. Keep in mind, that true Bible belief has actions. So all things are possible to those that act like God's Word is true.

Impossible situations and still conceiving.

In this portion of the book I want to deal especially with the more impossible situations. You can take a field of concrete and have the best of crops on it by sowing a lot of seeds. The seeds you keep putting on the concrete will finally build up a soil bed that will be one of the best, if not the best soil beds for conceiving those seeds.

In Mark 4 Jesus taught that His words were seeds. Not long after in Mark 11, Jesus then demonstrated how to use His words as seeds. Jesus spoke to a perfectly live tree and told it to die. (Note: Jesus wasn't mean, even to trees. If you will study the nature of this tree it wasn't any good.) The tree did not look any different at all. However, after at least a day later the tree had dried up from the roots (Mark 11:20). In verse 21, Peter remembered Jesus cursing the fig tree and said, "Behold (this word in the Greek co-equally is rendered "look as in surprise")…. Jesus knew that the disciples were astonished so He explained to them how they could do the same thing. Verse 21….He told them, all they needed was to have faith in God. Another translation says, "Have the God kind of faith". Then the very next verse (23) Jesus told them how they could have exactly the same kind of faith that God has. Or to have faith in God and they (or we) can do the same thing. Simply say or speak in agreement with God's Word three times more than you believe.

Some people have a real HARD time doing these steps of receiving. That simply means their heart has an area which is hard, like the concrete field. I am not saying this to condemn any one. Every one has areas that are easier for them to believe for and other areas that are harder to believe for. If you have an area that seems HARD, find a lot of Scriptures to validate God wants that for you. Then keep speaking it. There are even some areas in my life that I have spoken God's Word for many, many years before I conceived.

Just as a woman that is in the early stages of pregnancy, she does not care what any one says or thinks. She knows she has conceived and she knows she is going to have what that seed is suppose to produce. If you follow the laws of conception one of these days you will KNOW you have conceived and you KNOW you are going to have. I've been told that when a man and woman that are in Holy matrimony come together desiring to conceive a child that there is enough seed sown for every woman in the U.S. to conceive. They may come together for six months or a year before there is a conception. So the laws of sowing are extremely large in some cases. However, once you conceived, you KNOW you are going to HAVE!

Other books by Mel Bond:

Understanding Your Worst Enemy
Releasing God's Anointing
Neglecting Signs and Wonders is Neglecting the Rapture
Unimaginable Love

For a complete list of teaching tapes and books write:

Agape Church
140 N. Point Prairie
Wentzville, MO 63385

Music CD by Donna Bond: *Come Up Higher*